To

....

From

Glenda S. Winchester KWA6C

Date

....

Footprints

A *Pocket Inspirations* Book

summerside
PRESS

Summerside Press
Minneapolis, MN 55337
www.summersidepress.com

Footprints

A *Pocket Inspirations* Book
© 2011 Summerside Press

ISBN 978-1-60936-367-3

Scripture references are from the following sources: The Holy Bible, King James Version (KJV). The Holy Bible, New International Version®, NIV®. Copyright © 1973, 1978, 1984, 2011 by Biblica, Inc.™ Used by permission of Zondervan. All rights reserved worldwide. The New King James Version (NKJV). Copyright © 1982 by Thomas Nelson, Inc. Used by permission. The New American Standard Bible® (NASB), Copyright © 1960, 1962, 1963, 1968, 1971, 1972, 1973, 1975, 1977, 1995 by The Lockman Foundation. Used by permission. The Holy Bible, New Living Translation (NLT), copyright 1996, 2004. Used by permission of Tyndale House Publishers, Inc., Wheaton, Illinois. *The Message* (MSG). Copyright © 1993, 1994, 1995, 1996, 2000, 2001, 2002 by Eugene Peterson. Used by permission of NavPress, Colorado Springs, CO. All rights reserved. The Holy Bible, English Standard Version® (ESV), copyright © 2001 by Crossway Bibles, a publishing ministry of Good News Publishers. Used by permission.

Compiled by Jill Jones
Designed by Lisa & Jeff Franke

Summerside Press™ is an inspirational publisher offering fresh, irresistible books to uplift the heart and engage the mind.

Printed in USA.

Contents

Footprints in the Sand

One night I dreamed I was walking
Along the beach with the Lord.
Many scenes from my life flashed across the sky.
In each scene I noticed footprints in the sand.
Sometimes there were two sets of footprints.
Other times there was one set of footprints.
This bothered me because I noticed that
During the low periods of my life when I was
Suffering from anguish, sorrow, or defeat,
I could see only one set of footprints,
So I said to the Lord, "You promised me,
Lord, that if I followed You,
You would walk with me always.
But I noticed that during the most trying periods
Of my life there have only been
One set of prints in the sand.
Why, when I have needed You most,
You have not been there for me?"
The Lord replied,
"The times when you have seen only one set of footprints
Is when I carried you."

Ella H. Scharring Hausen

Introduction

In the midst of loneliness, fear, or uncertainty,
when the pain of life comes crashing in and
we wonder where God is, the timeless words of
"Footprints" stand as a reminder that God
will never leave us or forsake us.

In this *Pocket Inspirations* book, the much-loved
poem has been divided into nine parts. Each
part serves as the inspiration for chapters in
which you'll find encouragement from Scripture
and quotations by men and women whose words
will touch your heart. So you can check the table
of contents and select the topic that you most
identify with, then turn to that chapter and feel
your heart comforted and strengthened as you
read, or you can simply open the book at
random and read at your leisure.

However you choose to use this book, may
the message of "Footprints" reassure your heart
and give you strength for the journey!

ONE

I Walk with God

One night I dreamed I was walking
Along the beach with the Lord.

ELLA H. SCHARRING-HAUSEN

When I walk by the wayside,
He is along with me....
Amid all my forgetfulness of Him,
He never forgets me.

THOMAS CHALMERS

He has shown you, O mortal, what is good.
And what does the LORD require of you?
To act justly and to love mercy and to
walk humbly with your God.

MICAH 6:8 NIV

May your life become one of glad and unending
praise to the Lord as you journey through this
world, and in the world that is to come!

TERESA OF AVILA

All the way to heaven is heaven begun
to the Christian who walks near enough to God
to hear the secrets He has to impart.

E. M. BOUNDS

Joy is more than my spontaneous expression
of laughter, gaiety, and lightness. It is deeper
than an emotional expression of happiness.
Joy is a growing, evolving manifestation of
God in my life as I walk with Him.

BONNIE MONSON

And He walks with me, and He talks with me,
And He tells me I am His own.
And the joy we share as we tarry there
None other has ever known.

C. AUSTIN MILES

The LORD is my shepherd;
I have all that I need.
He lets me rest in green meadows;
he leads me beside peaceful streams.
He renews my strength.
He guides me along right paths.

PSALM 23:1–3 NLT

God wants nothing from us except our needs,
and these furnish Him with room to display
His bounty when He supplies them freely....
Not what I have, but what I do not have, is the
first point of contact between my soul and God.

CHARLES H. SPURGEON

Take your everyday, ordinary life—your sleeping,
eating, going-to-work, and walking-around life—
and place it before God as an offering.

ROMANS 12:1 MSG

Whoever walks toward God one step,
God runs toward him two.

JEWISH PROVERB

Jesus wants to live His life in you,
to look through your eyes, walk with your feet,
love with your heart.

MOTHER TERESA

Love the LORD your God, walk in all his ways,
obey his commands, hold firmly to him, and
serve him with all your heart and all your soul.

JOSHUA 22:5 NLT

May your footsteps set you upon a lifetime
journey of love. May you wake each day with
His blessings and sleep each night in His keeping.
And may you always walk in His tender care.

Walk in all the way that the LORD your God
has commanded you, so that you may live
and prosper and prolong your days.

DEUTERONOMY 5:33 NIV

When I look at the galaxies on a clear night—
when I look at the incredible brilliance
of creation, and think that this is what
God is like, then instead of feeling intimidated
and diminished by it, I am enlarged—
I rejoice that I am part of it.

MADELEINE L'ENGLE

How beautiful it is to be alive!
To wake each morn as if the Maker's grace
Did us afresh from nothingness derive.

HENRY SEPTIMUS SUTTON

Above all give me grace to use these beauties
of earth without me and this eager stirring
of life within me as a means whereby my soul
may rise from creature to Creator,
and from nature to nature's God.

JOHN BAILLIE

You will reach your destination
if you walk with God.

I believe that nothing that happens to me is
meaningless, and that it is good for us all that it
should be so, even if it runs counter to our own
wishes. As I see it, I'm here for some purpose,
and I only hope I may fulfill it.

DIETRICH BONHOEFFER

God has a purpose for your life
and no one else can take your place.

Call to Me, and I will answer you, and show you
great and mighty things, which you do not know.

JEREMIAH 33:3 NKJV

To everything there is a season,
a time for every purpose under heaven.

ECCLESIASTES 3:1 NKJV

If you believe in God, it is not too difficult to
believe that He is concerned about the universe
and all the events on this earth. But the really
staggering message of the Bible is that this same
God cares deeply about you and your identity
and the events of your life.

BRUCE LARSON

The LORD directs the steps of the godly.
He delights in every detail of their lives.
Though they stumble, they will never fall,
for the LORD holds them by the hand.

PSALM 37:23-24 NLT

Thank God that even when we are not worthy
of His blessings, He still loves us and bestows
peace, joy, and happiness.

GARY SMALLEY AND JOHN TRENT

And we know that all things work together
for good to those who love God, to those who
are the called according to His purpose.

ROMANS 8:28 NKJV

The meaning of earthly existence lies,
not as we have grown used to thinking,
in prospering, but in the
development of the soul.

ALEKSANDR SOLZHENITSYN

We don't have to be perfect to be a blessing.
We are asked only to be real, trusting in His
perfection to cover our imperfection, knowing
that one day we will finally be all that Christ
saved us for and wants us to be.

GIGI GRAHAM TCHIVIDJIAN

The LORD watches over those who fear him,
those who rely on his unfailing love.

PSALM 33:18 NLT

Lord, hear my prayer. When I stumble over my
words, or when I can't find the right words to say,
listen to my heart. I want to talk with You.
I want to walk with You. Hear me, O Lord, and
answer with grace and love and mercy.
Take my hand and my heart and lead me.

MARILYN JANSEN

God's hand is always there; once you grasp it
you'll never want to let it go.

The crucified Christ is the One who
comes to walk with us every day.

ANDREW MURRAY

What is important is that you are holding on,
that you have got a grip on Christ
and He will not let your hand go.

MOTHER TERESA

I'm still in your presence, but you've taken my
hand. You wisely and tenderly lead me,
and then you bless me.

PSALM 73:21 MSG

The Lord's goodness surrounds us at every
moment. I walk through it almost with difficulty,
as through thick grass and flowers.

R. W. BARBER

How vital that we pray, armed with the
knowledge that God is in heaven.... Spend some
time walking in the workshop of the heavens,
seeing what God has done, and watch how your
prayers are energized.

MAX LUCADO

Real help comes from GOD.
Your blessing clothes your people!

PSALM 3:8 MSG

God bless you and utterly satisfy
your heart...with Himself.

AMY CARMICHAEL

Be sure to remember that nothing in your daily
life is so insignificant and so inconsequential that
God will not help you by answering your prayer.

OLE HALLESBY

Be assured, if you walk with Him
and look to Him and expect help from Him,
He will never fail you.

GEORGE MUELLER

Call on me in the day of trouble;
I will deliver you, and you will honor me.

PSALM 50:15 NIV

Jesus Christ has brought every need, every joy,
every gratitude, every hope of ours
before God. He accompanies us and brings us
into the presence of God.

DIETRICH BONHOEFFER

I call on you, O God, for you will answer me;
give ear to me and hear my prayer.

PSALM 17:6 NIV

If you are walking in darkness, without a ray of
light, trust in the LORD and rely on your God.

ISAIAH 50:10 NLT

One took my hand at the entrance dim,
And sweet is the road that I walk with Him.

L. B. COWMAN

It is better to walk in the dark with
God than to walk alone in the light.

THE STILL SMALL VOICE

Trust in the LORD with all your heart;
do not depend on your own understanding.
Seek his will in all you do,
and he will show you which path to take.

PROVERBS 3:5-6 NLT

God still draws near to us in the ordinary,
commonplace, everyday experiences
and places.... He comes in surprising ways.

HENRY GARIEPY

The LORD bless you and keep you;
The LORD make His face shine upon you,
And be gracious to you;
The LORD lift up His countenance upon you,
And give you peace.

NUMBERS 6:24–26 NKJV

Have you ever thought that in every action
of grace in your heart you have the whole
omnipotence of God engaged to bless you?

ANDREW MURRAY

May the favor of the Lord our God rest on us;
establish the work of our hands for us—
yes, establish the work of our hands.

PSALM 90:17 NIV

Trust the Lord!
He is your helper and your shield.

PSALM 115:9 NLT

I saw Him in the morning light,
He made the day shine clear and bright;
I saw Him in the noontide hour,
And gained from Him refreshing shower....
I saw Him when great losses came,
And found He loved me just the same.
When heavy loads I had to bear,
I found He lightened every care....
For as each day unfolds its light,
We'll walk by faith and not by sight.
Life will, indeed, a blessing bring,
If we see God in everything.

A. E. FINN

As you continue holding [on], you will discover
that God has a magnetic attracting quality!
Your God is like a magnet! The Lord naturally
draws you more and more toward Himself.

MADAME JEANNE GUYON

TWO

God's Presence Is with Me

*Many scenes from my life flashed across the sky.
In each scene I noticed footprints in the sand.*

ELLA H. SCHARRING-HAUSEN

We are always in the presence of God....
There is never a nonsacred moment!
His presence never diminishes. Our awareness
of His presence may falter, but the reality
of His presence never changes.

MAX LUCADO

This is how we experience his deep and abiding
presence in us: by the Spirit he gave us.

1 JOHN 3:24 MSG

I lift my eyes to you, O God,
enthroned in heaven.
We keep looking to the LORD our God
for his mercy.

PSALM 123:1–2 NLT

God is the sunshine that warms us, the rain
that melts the frost and waters the young
plants. The presence of God is a climate
of strong and bracing love, always there.

JOAN ARNOLD

Where morning dawns, where evening fades,
you call forth songs of joy.

PSALM 65:8 NIV

There is an essential connection between
experiencing God, loving God, and trusting
God. You will trust God only as much
as you love Him, and you will love Him
to the extent you have touched Him,
rather that He has touched you.

BRENNAN MANNING

Much of what is sacred is hidden in the ordinary,
everyday moments of our lives. To see something
of the sacred in those moments takes slowing
down so we can live our lives more reflectively.

KEN GIRE

Within each of us there is an inner place
where the living God Himself longs to dwell,
our sacred center of belief.

Although it [is] good to think upon
the kindness of God, and to love Him
and worship Him for it; yet it is far better
to gaze upon the pure essence of Him and
to love Him and worship Him for Himself.

We desire many things, and God offers
us only one thing. He can offer us only
one thing—Himself. He has nothing else to give.
There is nothing else to give.

PETER KREEFT

Forbid that I should walk through Thy beautiful
world with unseeing eyes: Forbid that the lure
of the market-place should ever entirely steal
my heart away from the love of the open
acres and the green trees: Forbid that under the
low roof of workshop or office or study I should
ever forget Thy great overarching sky.

JOHN BAILLIE

The God who holds the whole world in His
hands wraps Himself in the splendor of the sun's
light and walks among the clouds.

Savor little glimpses of God's goodness
and His majesty, thankful for the gift of them.

There is nothing but God's grace. We walk upon
it; we breathe it; we live and die by it; it makes
the nails and axles of the universe.

ROBERT LOUIS STEVENSON

LORD, our Lord,
how majestic is your name in all the earth!
You have set your glory in the heavens....
When I consider your heavens,
the work of your fingers,
the moon and the stars,
which you have set in place,
what is mankind that you are mindful of them,
human beings that you care for them?
You made them a little lower than the angels
and crowned them with glory and honor....
O LORD, our Lord,
how majestic is your name in all the earth!

PSALM 8:1, 3–5, 9 NIV

The longer I live, the more my mind dwells upon
the beauty and the wonder of the world.

JOHN BURROUGHS

Dear friends, let us continue to love one another,
for love comes from God. Anyone who loves
is a child of God and knows God.

1 JOHN 4:7 NLT

You will find as you look back upon your life,
that the moments when you have really
lived are the moments when you have done
things in the spirit of love.

HENRY DRUMMOND

Let us consider how we may spur one another
on toward love and good deeds...encouraging
one another—and all the more
as you see the Day approaching.

HEBREWS 10:24–25 NIV

We are simply human beings, enfolded in
weakness and in hope, called together to change
our world one heart at a time!

JEAN VANIER

When we focus on God, the scene changes.
He's in control of our lives; nothing lies
outside the realm of His redemptive grace.
Even when we make mistakes,
fail in relationships, or deliberately make
bad choices, God can redeem us.

PENELOPE J. STOKES

The LORD is compassionate and gracious,
slow to anger, abounding in love.

PSALM 103:8 NIV

You can never change the past. But by the grace
of God, you can win the future. So remember
those things which will help you forward, but
forget those things which will only hold you back.

RICHARD C. WOODSOME

How precious to me are your thoughts, God!
How vast is the sum of them! Were I to count
them, they would outnumber the grains of sand.

PSALM 139:17–18 NIV

Although mementos can be preserved
or displayed behind glass, memories live on
in the heart, where they deepen and resonate
over the years, providing strength
and comfort in times of need.

Look to the LORD and his strength; seek his face
always. Remember the wonders he has done.

PSALM 105:4–5 NIV

Memory is history recorded in our brain;
memory is a painter, it paints pictures
of the past and of the day.

GRANDMA MOSES

I will remember the works of the LORD;
Surely I will remember Your wonders of old.
I will also meditate on all Your work,
And talk of Your deeds.

PSALM 77:11–12 NKJV

The space between yesterday and today
is filled with acceptance,
forgiveness and remembering to laugh.

The heavens declare the glory of God;
And the firmament shows His handiwork.

PSALM 19:1 NKJV

If we are children of God, we have
a tremendous treasure in nature
and will realize that it is holy and sacred.
We will see God reaching out to us
in every wind that blows, every sunrise
and sunset, every cloud in the sky, every flower
that blooms, and every leaf that fades.

OSWALD CHAMBERS

Look up at all the stars in the night sky
and hear your Father saying, "I carefully set each
one in its place. Know that I love you more than
these." Sit by the lake's edge, listening to the
water lapping the shore and hear your Father
gently calling you to that place near His heart.

WENDY MOORE

The God who flung from His fingertips this
universe filled with galaxies and stars...is the God
who loves with magnificent monotony.

BRENNAN MANNING

One of the great secrets for growing up
in Christ is to remember that whether
we're riding a bus or working in the office
or washing dishes at home or playing
a game of golf, Jesus Christ is there.

LEIGHTON FORD

Beauty puts a face on God. When we gaze
at nature, at a loved one, at a work of art,
our soul immediately recognizes
and is drawn to the face of God.

MARGARET BROWNLEY

Whom have I in heaven but You?
And besides You, I desire nothing on earth.
My flesh and my heart may fail,
But God is the strength of my heart
and my portion forever....
As for me, the nearness of God is my good;
I have made the Lord GOD my refuge.

PSALM 73:25–26, 28 NASB

God is not only the answer to a thousand needs,
He is the answer to a thousand wants.
He is the fulfillment of our chief desire
in all of life. For whether or not we've ever
recognized it, what we desire is unfailing love.
Oh, God, awake our souls to see—You are what
we want, not just what we need. Yes, our life's
protection, but also our heart's affection. Yes, our
soul's salvation, but also our heart's exhilaration.
Unfailing love. A love that will not let me go!

BETH MOORE

The peace of God must quiet our minds and rest
our hearts. We must put our hand in the hand
of God like a little child, and let Him lead us out
into the bright sunshine of His love.

PARDINGTON

You are precious in my eyes,
and honored, and I love you.

ISAIAH 43:4 ESV

Live in me. Make your home in me just
as I do in you.... If you make yourselves
at home with me and my words are at home
in you, you can be sure that whatever you ask
will be listened to and acted upon.... I've loved
you the way my Father has loved me.
Make yourselves at home in my love.

JOHN 15:4, 7, 9 MSG

The greatest honor we can give God is to live
gladly because of the knowledge of His love.

JULIAN OF NORWICH

I will remember that when I give Him my heart,
God chooses to live within me—body and soul.
And I know He really is as close as breathing,
His very Spirit inside of me.

How blessed is the one whom You choose
and bring near to You to dwell in Your courts.

PSALM 65:4 NASB

The impetus of God's love comes from within
Himself, to share with us His life and love.
It is a beautiful, eternal gift, held out to us in the
hands of love. All we have to do is say "Yes!"

JOHN POWELL

Great is his love toward us, and the faithfulness
of the LORD endures forever.

PSALM 117:2 NIV

"God has for Christ's sake loved us." Think of
it! We are loved eternally, totally, individually,
unreservedly! Nothing can take God's love away.

GLORIA GAITHER

In some way or other we will have to learn
the difference between trusting in the gift and
trusting in the Giver. The gift may be good
for a while, but the Giver is the Eternal Love.

F. B. MEYER

God is with us in the midst of our daily, routine
lives. In the middle of cleaning the house or
driving somewhere in the pickup.... Often it's in
the middle of the most mundane task that He
lets us know He is there with us. We realize, then,
that there can be no "ordinary" moments for
people who live their lives with Jesus.

MICHAEL CARD

The Word became human and made his home
among us. He was full of unfailing love
and faithfulness. And we have seen his glory,
the glory of the Father's one and only Son.

JOHN 1:14 NLT

We encounter God in the ordinariness
of life, not in the search for spiritual highs
and extraordinary, mystical experiences,
but in our simple presence in life.

BRENNAN MANNING

THREE

I Am Never Alone

Sometimes there were two sets of footprints.

ELLA H. SCHARRING-HAUSEN

We are not alone on our journey.
The God of love who gave us life sent us
[His] only Son to be with us at all times
and in all places, so that we never have
to feel lost in our struggles but always
can trust that God walks with us.

HENRI J. M. NOUWEN

Draw near to God and He will draw near to you.

JAMES 4:8 NASB

The LORD is close to the brokenhearted;
he rescues those whose spirits are crushed.

PSALM 34:18 NLT

I have sought Thy nearness;
With all my heart have I called Thee,
And going out to meet Thee
I found Thee coming toward me.

YEHUDA HALEVI

It is not objective proof of God's existence that
we want but, whether we use religious language
for it or not, the experience of God's presence.
That is the miracle we are really after. And that
is also, I think, the miracle that we really get.

FREDERICK BUECHNER

You are never alone. In your heart of hearts,
in the place where no two people are ever alike,
Christ is waiting for you. And what you never
dared hope for springs to life.

ROGER OF TAIZÉ

By entering through faith into what God has
always wanted to do for us...we have it all
together with God because of our Master
Jesus.... We throw open our doors to God
and discover at the same moment that he has
already thrown open his door to us.

ROMANS 5:1–2 MSG

Do you believe that God is near?
He wants you to. He wants you to know that
He is in the midst of your world.
Wherever you are as you read these words,
He is present.
In your car. On the plane. In your office,
your bedroom, your den.
He's near. And He is more than near.
He is active.

MAX LUCADO

He...guided them by the skillfulness of his hands.

PSALM 78:72 NKJV

Let all who take refuge in you rejoice;
let them ever sing for joy,
and spread your protection over them,
that those who love your name
may exult in you.

PSALM 5:11 ESV

You are in the Beloved...therefore infinitely
dear to the Father, unspeakably precious to Him.
You are never, not for one second, alone.

NORMAN DOWTY

It is God to whom and with whom we travel,
and while He is the End of our journey,
He is also at every stopping place.

ELISABETH ELLIOT

I will lead them home with great care.
They will walk beside quiet streams and on
smooth paths where they will not stumble.

JEREMIAH 31:9 NLT

He will rescue you from every trap
and protect you from deadly disease.
He will cover you with his feathers.
He will shelter you with his wings.
His faithful promises are your
armor and protection.
Do not be afraid of the terrors of the night,
nor the arrow that flies in the day.
Do not dread the disease that stalks in darkness,
nor the disaster that strikes at midday....
If you make the LORD your refuge,
if you make the Most High your shelter,
no evil will conquer you....
The LORD says, "I will rescue those who love me.
I will protect those who trust in my name."

PSALM 91:3–6, 9–10, 14 NLT

When you take the first step to embrace
God in your circumstances, He will go
the distance to embrace you.

STORMIE OMARTIAN

God did not tell us to follow Him because
He needed our help, but because He knew
that loving Him would make us whole.

IRENAEUS

God made my life complete when I placed
all the pieces before him.... GOD rewrote
the text of my life when I opened the book
of my heart to his eyes.

PSALM 18:20, 24 MSG

The "air" which our souls need also envelops
all of us at all times and on all sides.
God is round about us in Christ on every hand,
with many-sided and all-sufficient grace.
All we need to do is to open our hearts.

OLE HALLESBY

I look behind me and you're there,
then up ahead and you're there, too—
your reassuring presence, coming and going.

PSALM 139:5 MSG

Have confidence in God's mercy,
for when you think He is a long way from you,
He is often quite near.

THOMAS À KEMPIS

When God finds a soul that rests in Him
and is not easily moved...to this same soul
He gives the joy of His presence.

CATHERINE OF GENOA

We need never shout across the spaces to an
absent God. He is nearer than our own soul,
closer than our most secret thoughts.

A. W. TOZER

God is always present in the temple of your
heart...His home. And when you come in to
meet Him there, you find that it is the one place
of deep satisfaction where every longing is met.
Always be in a state of expectancy, and see that
you leave room for God to come in as He likes.

OSWALD CHAMBERS

I don't know what the future holds,
but I know who holds the future.

E. STANLEY JONES

Trust the past to the mercy of God, the present
to His love, and the future to His Providence.

AUGUSTINE

What is the Lord saying? There's only one
message: "Trust Me. Even when you don't
understand and can't comprehend: trust Me!"

JAMES DOBSON

You can trust God right now to supply all your
needs for today. And if your needs are more
tomorrow, His supply will be greater also.

How could I be anything but quite happy
if I believed always that all the past is forgiven,
and all the present furnished with power,
and all the future bright with hope.

JAMES SMETHAM

God's love...is ever and always,
eternally present to all who fear him,
making everything right for them and their
children as they follow his Covenant ways.

PSALM 103:17–18 MSG

God wants to be wanted, to be wanted
enough that we are *ready*, predisposed
to find Him present with us.

DALLAS WILLARD

God loves to look at us, and loves it when
we will look back at Him. Even when we try
to run away from our troubles...God will find us,
bless us, when we feel most alone, unsure....
God will find a way to let us know that He is
with us in this place, wherever we are.

KATHLEEN NORRIS

When all is said and done, the last word
is Immanuel—God-With-Us.

ISAIAH 8:10 MSG

God gets down on His knees
among us; gets on our level and shares
Himself with us. He does not reside
afar off and send diplomatic messages,
He kneels among us.... God shares
Himself generously and graciously.

EUGENE PETERSON

Who shall separate us from the love
of Christ? Shall trouble or hardship
or persecution or famine or nakedness or
danger or sword?... No, in all these things
we are more than conquerors through
him who loved us. For I am convinced
that neither death nor life, neither angels
nor demons, neither the present nor
the future, nor any powers, neither
height nor depth, nor anything else
in all creation, will be able to separate
us from the love of God that
is in Christ Jesus our Lord.

ROMANS 8:35, 37–39 NIV

My Presence will go with you,
and I will give you rest.

EXODUS 33:14 NIV

When I feel most alone, I draw comfort from the
promise that nothing can separate me from
the love of Christ. Nothing. He is with me always.

My goal is God Himself, not joy, nor peace,
Nor even blessing, but Himself, my God.

L. B. COWMAN

All the paths of the LORD are lovingkindness
and truth to those who keep His covenant.

PSALM 25:10 NASB

God, who has led you safely on so far,
will lead you on to the end. Be altogether at rest
in the loving holy confidence which you ought
to have in His heavenly Providence.

FRANCIS DE SALES

It is God's will that we believe that we see
Him continually, though it seems to us that
the sight be only partial; and through this belief
He makes us always to gain more grace,
for God wishes to be seen, and He wishes
to be sought, and He wishes to be expected,
and He wishes to be trusted.

Seek the LORD your God, and you will
find Him if you seek Him with all your
heart and with all your soul.

DEUTERONOMY 4:29 NKJV

So faith bounds forward to its goal in God,
and love can trust her Lord to lead her there;
upheld by Him my soul is following hard,
till God hath full fulfilled my deepest prayer.

F. BROOK

Ask and you'll get; seek and you'll find; knock
and the door will open. Don't bargain with God.
Be direct. Ask for what you need.

LUKE 11:9–10 MSG

God longs to give favor—
that is, spiritual strength and health—
to those who seek Him, and Him alone.
He grants spiritual favors and victories,
not because the one who seeks Him
is holier than anyone else, but in order
to make His holy beauty and His great
redeeming power known.... For it is through
the living witness of others that we are
drawn to God at all. It is because of His
creatures, and His work in them,
that we come to praise Him.

TERESA OF AVILA

Guidance is a sovereign act. Not merely
does God will to guide us by showing us
His way...whatever mistakes we may make,
we shall come safely home. Slippings
and strayings there will be, no doubt,
but the everlasting arms are beneath us;
we shall be caught, rescued, restored.

J. I. PACKER

God has not promised us an easy journey,
but He has promised us a safe journey.

WILLIAM C. MILLER

God can pour on the blessings
in astonishing ways so that you're ready
for anything and everything, more than
just ready to do what needs to be done.

2 CORINTHIANS 9:8 MSG

The grace of God means something like:
Here is your life. You might never have been,
but you are because the party wouldn't have
been complete without you.
Here is the world. Beautiful and terrible things
will happen. Don't be afraid. I am with you.
Nothing can ever separate us. It's for you I
created the universe. I love you.

FREDERICK BUECHNER

The word of the LORD is right and true;
he is faithful in all he does.

PSALM 33:4 NIV

FOUR

God Is Always Good

*This bothered me because I noticed that
During the low periods of my life when I was
Suffering from anguish, sorrow, or defeat...*

ELLA H. SCHARRING-HAUSEN

God's ways seem dark, but soon or late,
They touch the shining hills of day.

JOHN GREENLEAF WHITTIER

Remember how the LORD your God led you
through the wilderness.... For the LORD
your God is bringing you into a good land
of flowing streams and pools of water.

DEUTERONOMY 8:2, 7 NLT

When we are in a situation where Jesus is all we have, we soon discover He is all we really need.

GIGI GRAHAM TCHIVIDJIAN

We're depending on GOD; he's everything we need. What's more, our hearts brim with joy since we've taken for our own his holy name.

PSALM 33:20 MSG

If you find yourself in this spiritual state feeling wayward, unstable in heart, confused... cling to the Lord in prayer! He always hears, and He will answer.

TERESA OF AVILA

When times get hard, remember Jesus.... When tears come, remember Jesus.... When fear pitches his tent in your front yard. When death looms, when anger singes, when shame weighs heavily. Remember Jesus.

MAX LUCADO

Then you will call, and the LORD will answer;
you will cry for help, and he will say: Here am I.

ISAIAH 58:9 NIV

There is a place of comfort sweet
Near to the heart of God,
A place where we our Savior meet,
Near to the heart of God....
Hold us who wait before Thee
Near to the heart of God.

CLELAND B. MCAFEE

Not a sigh is breathed, not a pain felt,
not a grief pierces the soul, but the throb
vibrates to the Father's heart.

ELLEN G. WHITE

Those who sow in tears shall reap in joy.

PSALM 126:5 NKJV

For the LORD God is our sun and our shield. He gives us grace and glory. The LORD will withhold no good thing from those who do what is right.

PSALM 84:11 NLT

After winter comes the summer.
After night comes the dawn. And after
every storm, there comes clear, open skies.

SAMUEL RUTHERFORD

Weak as we are
a strength beyond our strength has
pulled us through at least this far.

FREDERICK BUECHNER

He satisfies the thirsty and fills the hungry with good things.... He led them from the darkness and deepest gloom; he snapped their chains. Let them praise the LORD...for the wonderful things He has done for them.

PSALM 107:9, 14–15 NLT

Blessed be the God and Father of our Lord Jesus Christ, the Father of mercies and God of all comfort, who comforts us in all our affliction so that we will be able to comfort those who are in any affliction with the comfort with which we ourselves are comforted by God.

2 CORINTHIANS 1:3–4 NASB

Only God can truly comfort;
He comes alongside us and shows us how
deeply and tenderly He feels for us.

Grace...like the Lord, the Giver,
never fails from age to age.

JOHN NEWTON

Should we feel at times disheartened...,
a simple movement of heart toward God will
renew our powers. Whatever He may demand
of us, He will give us at the moment
the strength and courage that we need.

FRANÇOIS FÉNELON

He won't brush aside the bruised
and the hurt and he won't disregard
the small and insignificant.

ISAIAH 42:3 MSG

He shall gather the lambs with his arm, and
carry them in his bosom (Isaiah 40:11 NKJV).
Who is He of whom such gracious words
are spoken? He is the Good Shepherd.
Why does He carry the lambs in His bosom?
Because *He has a tender heart, and any weakness
at once melts His heart.* The sighs, the ignorance,
the feebleness of the little ones of His flock
draw forth His compassion.

The loving God we serve has immeasurable
compassion and tenderness toward
each of us throughout our lives.

JAMES DOBSON

I know not where His islands lift their
fronded palms in air; I only know I cannot drift
beyond His love and care.

JOHN GREENLEAF WHITTIER

Consider it pure joy, my brothers and sisters,
whenever you face trials of many kinds.

JAMES 1:2 NIV

Difficulties and obstacles are God's challenges
to faith. When hindrances confront us in the
path of duty, we are to recognize them
as vessels for faith to fill with the fullness and
all-sufficiency of Jesus; and as we go forward,
simply and fully trusting Him, we may be tested,
we may have to wait and let patience have her
perfect work; but we shall surely find at last
the stone rolled away and the Lord waiting
to render to us double for our time of testing.

A. B. SIMPSON

I have set the LORD always before me;
because he is at my right hand
I shall not be moved.

PSALM 16:8 KJV

Hear my cry, O God;
Give heed to my prayer.
From the end of the earth I call to You
when my heart is faint;
Lead me to the rock that is higher than I.
For You have been a refuge for me,
A tower of strength against the enemy.
Let me dwell in Your tent forever;
Let me take refuge in the shelter of Your wings.

PSALM 61:1–4 NASB

When God has become...our refuge
and our fortress, then we can reach out
to Him in the midst of a broken world
and feel at home while still on the way.

HENRI J. M. NOUWEN

Because of the LORD's great love
we are not consumed,
for his compassions never fail.
They are new every morning;
great is your faithfulness.

LAMENTATIONS 3:22-23 NIV

Our hearts were made for joy. Our hearts
were made to enjoy the One who created them.
Too deeply planted to be much affected
by the ups and downs of life, this joy is a
knowing and a being known by our Creator.
He sets our hearts alight with radiant joy.

WENDY MOORE

For you make me glad by your deeds, LORD;
I sing for joy at what your hands have done.

PSALM 92:4 NIV

If one is joyful, it means that one is faithfully
living for God and that nothing else counts;
and if one gives joy to others one is doing God's
work. With joy without and joy within, all is well.

JANET ERSKINE STUART

Splendor and majesty are before him;
strength and joy are in his dwelling place.

1 CHRONICLES 16:27 NIV

How blessed all those in whom you live,
  whose lives become roads you travel;
They wind through lonesome valleys,
come upon brooks, discover cool springs
  and pools brimming with rain!
  God-traveled, these roads curve
up the mountain, and at the last turn—
  Zion! God in full view!

PSALM 84:5–7 MSG

All our supply is to come from the Lord.
  Here are springs that shall never dry;
  here are fountains and streams
  that shall never be cut off. Here,
  anxious one, is the gracious pledge
  of the Heavenly Father. If He is the
  source of our mercies they can never
fail us. No heat, no drought can parch
  that river "the streams whereof
  make glad the city of God."

N. L. ZINZENDORF

The joy of the LORD is your strength.

NEHEMIAH 8:10 NLT

All God's glory and beauty come from within,
and there He delights to dwell.
His visits there are frequent, His conversation
sweet, His comforts refreshing,
His peace passing all understanding.

THOMAS À KEMPIS

Now may our Lord Jesus Christ Himself
and God our Father, who has loved us
and given us eternal comfort and good hope
by grace, comfort and strengthen your hearts
in every good work and word.

2 THESSALONIANS 2:16–17 NASB

God comforts. He lays His right hand
on the wounded soul...and He says, as if that
one were the only soul in all the universe:
O greatly beloved, fear not: peace be unto you.

AMY CARMICHAEL

Live for today but hold your hands open to tomorrow. Anticipate the future and its changes with joy. There is a seed of God's love in every event, every circumstance, every unpleasant situation in which you may find yourself.

BARBARA JOHNSON

All who listen to me will live in peace, untroubled by fear of harm.

PROVERBS 1:33 NLT

Life itself, every bit of health that we enjoy, every hour of liberty and free enjoyment... comes from the hand of God.

BILLY GRAHAM

My God shall supply all your need according to His riches in glory by Christ Jesus.

PHILIPPIANS 4:19 NKJV

My heart says of you, "Seek his face!"
Your face, LORD, I will seek.

PSALM 27:8 NIV

Do you have a place of shelter where you
seek only His face? Do you spend time in that
secret place? Have you given prayer the priority
it deserves? When you pray, remember it is the
Lord's face you seek.

CHARLES R. SWINDOLL

Remember it is the very time for faith to work
when sight ceases. The greater the difficulties,
the easier for faith; as long as there remain
certain natural prospects, faith does not get on
even as easily as where natural prospects fail.

GEORGE MÜELLER

I am with you always, even to the end of the age.

MATTHEW 28:20 NKJV

The Lord will work out his plans for my life—
for your faithful love, O LORD, endures forever.
Don't abandon me, for you made me.

PSALM 138:8 NLT

See God in everything, and God will calm
and color all that you see! It may be that
the circumstances of our sorrows will not
be removed, their condition will remain
unchanged; but if Christ, as Lord and Master
of our life, is brought into our grief and gloom,
"He will compass us about with songs of
deliverance" (Psalm 32:7 KJV). To see Him,
and to be sure that His wisdom cannot err,
His power cannot fail, His love can never
change; to know that even His direst dealings
with us are for our deepest spiritual gain,
is to be able to say, in the midst
of bereavement, sorrow, pain, and loss,
"The Lord gave, and the Lord has taken away;
blessed be the name of the Lord" (Job 1:21 KJV).

HANNAH WHITALL SMITH

FIVE

God Keeps His Promises

I could see only one set of footprints,
So I said to the Lord,
"You promised me, Lord…"

ELLA H. SCHARRING-HAUSEN

Great faith isn't the ability to believe long
and far into the misty future. It's simply taking
God at His word and taking the next step.

JONI EARECKSON TADA

Now faith is being sure of what we hope
for and certain of what we do not see.

HEBREWS 11:1 NIV

Faith is not exactly belief. One can believe
anything…it's an assent in the mind. But faith
is completely different. It's the actual active
engagement of *God* in one's personal life.

<small>BRIAN STILLER</small>

Let us draw near to God with a sincere
heart in full assurance of faith…. Let us hold
unswervingly to the hope we profess,
for he who promised is faithful.

<small>HEBREWS 10:22–23 NIV</small>

Faith goes up the stairs that love has made and
looks out the window which hope has opened.

<small>CHARLES H. SPURGEON</small>

You will keep in perfect peace those whose
minds are steadfast, because they trust in you.
Trust in the LORD forever, for the LORD,
the LORD himself, is the Rock eternal.

<small>ISAIAH 26:3–4 NIV</small>

Do not let your heart be troubled;
believe in God, believe also in Me.
In My Father's house are many
dwelling places; if it were not so,
I would have told you;
for I go to prepare a place for you.
If I go and prepare a place for you,
I will come again and receive
you to Myself, that where I am,
there you may be also....
I will not leave you as orphans;
I will come to you....
Peace I leave with you;
My peace I give to you;
not as the world gives do I give to you.
Do not let your heart
be troubled, nor let it be fearful.

JOHN 14:1–3, 18, 27 NASB

Yet I am always with you;
you hold me by my right hand.

PSALM 73:23 NIV

Let's praise His name! He is holy, He is almighty.
He is love. He brings hope, forgiveness, heart
cleansing, peace and power. He is our deliverer
and coming King. Praise His wonderful name!

LUCILLE M. LAW

It doesn't take a huge spotlight to draw
attention to how great our God is.
All it takes is for one committed person
to so let His light shine before men,
that a world lost in darkness welcomes the light.

GARY SMALLEY AND JOHN TRENT

Therefore, since we have been made
right in God's sight by faith, we have peace
with God because of what Jesus Christ
our Lord has done for us.

ROMANS 5:1 NLT

The God of peace gives perfect peace
to those whose hearts are stayed upon Him.

CHARLES H. SPURGEON

A new day rose upon me. It was as if another
sun had risen into the sky; the heavens were
indescribably brighter, and the earth fairer;
and that day has gone on brightening to the
present hour. I have known the other joys of
life...but it is certain that till we see God in
the world—God in the bright and boundless
universe—we never know the highest joy.

ORVILLE DEWEY

Into all our lives, in many simple, familiar,
homely ways, God infuses this element of joy
from the surprises of life, which unexpectedly
brighten our days, and fill our eyes with light.

SAMUEL LONGFELLOW

Not one word of all the good words which
the LORD your God spoke concerning you has
failed; all have been fulfilled for you,
not one of them has failed.

JOSHUA 23:14 NASB

Each time a rainbow appears, stretching
from one end of the sky to the other, it's God
renewing His promise. Each shade of color,
each facet of light displays the radiant
spectrum of God's love—a promise that life
can be new for each one of us.

Not one word has failed of all His good promise.

1 KINGS 8:56 NASB

We may...depend upon God's promises, for...
He will be as good as His word. He is so kind
that He cannot deceive us, so true that He
cannot break His promise.

MATTHEW HENRY

Swim through your troubles.
Run to the promises, they are our Lord's
branches hanging over the water so that
His children may take a grip of them.

SAMUEL RUTHERFORD

Remember your promise to me;
it is my only hope.
Your promise revives me;
it comforts me in all my troubles....
Your eternal word, O LORD,
stands firm in heaven.
Your faithfulness extends to every generation,
as enduring as the earth you created.

PSALM 119:49–50, 89–90 NLT

O Lord, Your promise to never leave
my side helps keep me near You.
Come and fill me with your love.

MARILYN JANSEN

In keeping with his promise we are looking
forward to a new heaven and a new earth.

2 PETER 3:13 NIV

God has not promised skies always blue,
flower-strewn pathways all our lives through;
God has not promised sun without rain,
joy without sorrow, peace without pain.
But God has promised strength for the day,
rest for the labor, light for the way,
grace for the trials, help from above,
unfailing sympathy, undying love.

ANNIE JOHNSON FLINT

God's promises are like the stars;
the darker the night the brighter they shine.

DAVID NICHOLAS

The LORD always keeps his promises;
he is gracious in all he does.
The LORD helps the fallen
and lifts those bent beneath their loads.
The eyes of all look to you in hope....
The LORD is righteous in everything he does;
he is filled with kindness.
The LORD is close to all who call on him,
yes, to all who call on him in truth.

PSALM 145:13–15, 17–18 NLT

Faith in God is not blind. It is based
on His character and His promises.

Your promises have been thoroughly tested;
that is why I love them so much.

PSALM 119:140 NLT

For as the rain comes down, and the snow from
heaven, and do not return there, but water the
earth, and make it bring forth and bud, that
it may give seed to the sower and bread to the
eater, so shall My word be that goes forth from
My mouth; it shall not return to Me void, but
it shall accomplish what I please, and it shall
prosper in the thing for which I sent it.

ISAIAH 55:10–11 NKJV

God is the God of promise. He keeps His word,
even when that seems impossible.

COLIN URQUHART

The fulfillment of God's promise depends
entirely on trusting God and his way,
and then simply embracing him and what
he does. God's promise arrives as pure gift.

ROMANS 4:16 MSG

God's touch...lights the world with color
and renews our hearts with life.

JANET L. WEAVER SMITH

Brightness of my Father's glory,
Sunshine of my Father's face,
Let Your glory e'er shine on me,
Fill me with Your grace.

JEAN SOPIAN PIGOTT

Every good and perfect gift is from above,
coming down from the Father of the heavenly
lights, who does not change like shifting shadows.

JAMES 1:17 NIV

There are times, and there will be times,
when it will be absolutely clear that only
God's grace keeps us from falling apart;
and even if we cannot hold on to Him,
He will still hold on to us.

JOHANNES FACIUS

I will praise you, Lord,
among the nations;
I will sing of you among the peoples.
For great is your love,
reaching to the heavens;
your faithfulness reaches to the skies.
Be exalted, O God, above the heavens;
let your glory be over all the earth.

PSALM 57:9–11 NIV

In the morning, O LORD,
You will hear my voice; in the morning I will
order my prayer to You and eagerly watch.

PSALM 5:3 NASB

Always new. Always exciting.
Always full of promise.
The mornings of our lives,
each a personal daily miracle!

GLORIA GAITHER

With God, life is eternal—both in quality
and length. There is no joy comparable to the
joy of discovering something new from God,
about God. If the continuing life is a life of joy,
we will go on discovering, learning.

EUGENIA PRICE

That is God's call to us—simply to be people
who are content to live close to Him
and to renew the kind of life in which
the closeness is felt and experienced.

THOMAS MERTON

A quiet morning with a loving God
puts the events of the upcoming day
into proper perspective.

JANETTE OKE

Satisfy us in the morning with your
unfailing love, that we may sing for joy
and be glad all our days.

PSALM 90:14 NIV

In Your hand is power and might;
In Your hand it is to make great
And to give strength to all.

1 CHRONICLES 29:12 NKJV

Our feelings do not affect God's facts.
They may blow up, like clouds, and cover the
eternal things that we do most truly believe.
We may not see the shining of the promises—
but they still shine! [His strength] is not for one
moment less because of our human weakness.

AMY CARMICHAEL

In his kindness God called you to share in his
eternal glory by means of Christ Jesus.
So after you have suffered a little while,
he will restore, support, and strengthen you,
and he will place you on a firm foundation.

1 PETER 5:10 NLT

God promises to keep us in the palm of His
hand, with or without our awareness.
God has already made a space for us,
even if we have not made a space for God.

DAVID AND BARBARA SORENSEN

God...holds your entire life—
body and soul—in his hands.

LUKE 12:5 MSG

Into Your hands, O Lord, we commend
ourselves this day. Let Your presence
be with us to its close. Strengthen us to
remember that in whatsoever good work
we do we are serving You. Give us a diligent
and watchful spirit, that we may seek in
all things to know Your will, and knowing it,
gladly to perform it, to the honor and glory
of Your name; through Jesus Christ our Lord.

GELASIAN SACRAMENTARY

Create in me a clean heart, O God,
and renew a steadfast spirit within me.

PSALM 51:10 NKJV

The full power of the Word lies...in its
transforming power that does its divine work
as we listen. It is a word to heal us through,
and in, our listening here and now.

HENRI J. M. NOUWEN

Anyone who belongs to Christ has become a new
person. The old life is gone; a new life has begun!

2 CORINTHIANS 5:17 NLT

To pray is to change. This is a great grace.
How good of God to provide a path whereby
our lives can be taken over by love and joy and
peace and patience and kindness and goodness
and faithfulness and gentleness and self-control.

RICHARD J. FOSTER

A life transformed by the power of God
is always a marvel and a miracle.

GERALDINE NICHOLAS

For God is, indeed, a wonderful Father
who longs to pour out His mercy upon us,
and whose majesty is so great that He can
transform us from deep within.

TERESA OF AVILA

Be transformed by the renewing of your mind,
that you may prove what is that good and
acceptable and perfect will of God.

ROMANS 12:2 NKJV

Know therefore that the LORD your God is
God, the faithful God who keeps covenant and
steadfast love with those who love him and keep
his commandments, to a thousand generations.

DEUTERONOMY 7:9 ESV

Behold, I have inscribed you
on the palms of My hands.

ISAIAH 49:16 NASB

From eternity to eternity I am God.
No one can snatch anyone out of my hand.
No one can undo what I have done.

ISAIAH 43:13 NLT

Jesus Christ opens wide the doors of the treasure
house of God's promises, and bids us go in and
take with boldness the riches that are ours.

CORRIE TEN BOOM

Every day we live is a priceless gift of God,
loaded with possibilities to learn something new,
to gain fresh insights.

DALE EVANS ROGERS

SIX

God Always Walks with Me

"You promised me, Lord, that if I followed You, You would walk with me always..."

ELLA H. SCHARRING-HAUSEN

Faith is meant to be lived moment by moment. It isn't some broad, general outline—it's a long walk with a real Person.

JONI EARECKSON TADA

I would rather walk with God in the dark than go alone in the light.

MARY GARDINER BRAINARD

My Lord God, I have no idea where
I am going. I do not see the road ahead of me.
I cannot know for certain where it will end....
But I believe that the desire to please You
does in fact please You. And I hope
I have that desire in all that I am doing.
I hope that I will never do anything apart
from that desire. And I know that if I do this,
You will lead me by the right road though
I may know nothing about it. Therefore will
I trust You always though I may seem to be lost
and in the shadow of death. I will not fear,
for You are ever with me. And You will never
leave me to face my perils alone.

THOMAS MERTON

The best things are nearest:
breath in your nostrils, light in your eyes,
flowers at your feet, duties at your hand,
the path of God just before you.

ROBERT LOUIS STEVENSON

To You, O LORD, I lift up my soul.
O my God, in You I trust....
Make me know Your ways,
O LORD; teach me Your paths.
Lead me in Your truth and teach me,
for You are the God of my salvation;
for You I wait all the day.
Remember, O LORD, Your compassion
and Your lovingkindnesses,
for they have been from of old.

PSALM 25:1–2, 4–6 NASB

The Lord is able to guide. The promises
cover every imaginable situation....
Take the hand He stretches out.

ELISABETH ELLIOT

Only God gives true peace—a quiet gift
He sets within us just when we think we've
exhausted our search for it.

We are of such value to God that He came
to live among us...and to guide us home. He will
go to any length to seek us, even to being lifted
high upon the cross to draw us back to Himself.
We can only respond by loving God for His love.

CATHERINE OF SIENA

You guide me with your counsel,
leading me to a glorious destiny.

PSALM 73:24 NLT

For this God is our God for ever and ever;
he will be our guide even to the end.

PSALM 48:14 NIV

Your walk with God is essential. His heart
is not seen in an occasional chat or weekly visit.
We learn His will as we take up residence
in His house every single day.

MAX LUCADO

Those who know Your name will put
their trust in You; for You, LORD, have not
forsaken those who seek You.

PSALM 9:10 NKJV

God came to us because God wanted to join us
on the road, to listen to our story, and to help
us realize that we are not walking in circles but
moving toward the house of peace and joy.

HENRI J. M. NOUWEN

The thought of You stirs us so deeply that we
cannot be content unless we praise You, because
You have made us for Yourself and our hearts
find no peace until they rest in You.

AUGUSTINE

Surely goodness and mercy shall follow
me all the days of my life; and I will dwell
in the house of the LORD forever.

PSALM 23:6 NKJV

I'll take the hand of those
who don't know the way,
who can't see where they're going.
I'll be a personal guide to them,
directing them through unknown country.
I'll be right there to show them what
roads to take, make sure they don't fall
into the ditch. These are the things I'll be
doing for them—sticking with them,
not leaving them for a minute.

Isaiah 42:16 msg

Heaven often seems distant and unknown,
but if He who made the road...is our guide,
we need not fear to lose the way.

Henry van Dyke

Whether you turn to the right or to the left,
your ears will hear a voice behind you, saying,
"This is the way; walk in it."

Isaiah 30:21 niv

May God's love guide you through
the special plans He has for your life.

The LORD says, "I will guide you along
the best pathway for your life.
I will advise you and watch over you."

PSALM 32:8 NLT

I know that God is faithful.
I know that He answers prayers,
many times in ways I may not understand.

SHEILA WALSH

We can make our plans, but the LORD
determines our steps.

PROVERBS 16:9 NLT

Give me the peace that comes from
knowing that where I am, You are,
and together we can handle whatever comes.

PAM KIDD

O LORD, You are my God;
I will exalt You,
I will give thanks to Your name;
For You have worked wonders,
Plans formed long ago,
with perfect faithfulness.

ISAIAH 25:1 NASB

You, Lord, are a compassionate
and gracious God, slow to anger,
abounding in love and faithfulness.
Turn to me and have mercy on me.

PSALM 86:15–16 NIV

Let us, with a gladsome mind,
Praise the Lord, for He is kind:
For His mercies aye endure,
Ever faithful, ever sure.

JOHN MILTON

God takes care of His own. He knows
our needs. He anticipates our crises.
He is moved by our weaknesses. He stands
ready to come to our rescue. And at just
the right moment He steps in and proves
Himself as our faithful heavenly Father.

CHARLES R. SWINDOLL

I will declare that your love
stands firm forever, that you established
your faithfulness in heaven itself.

PSALM 89:2 NIV

God is a rich and bountiful Father,
and He does not forget His children,
nor withhold from them anything which
it would be to their advantage to receive.

J. K. MACLEAN

Let love and faithfulness never leave you;
bind them around your neck,
write them on the tablet of your heart.

PROVERBS 3:3 NIV

Bless the LORD, O my soul;
And all that is within me, bless His holy name!
Bless the LORD, O my soul,
And forget not all His benefits:
Who forgives all your iniquities,
Who heals all your diseases,
Who redeems your life from destruction,
Who crowns you with lovingkindness
and tender mercies,
Who satisfies your mouth with good things,
So that your youth is renewed like the eagle's.

PSALM 103:1–5 NKJV

God, who is love—who is, if I may say it
this way, made out of love—simply cannot
help but shed blessing on blessing upon us.

HANNAH WHITALL SMITH

I will send down showers in season;
there will be showers of blessing.

Ezekiel 34:26 niv

We benefit eternally by
God's being just what He is.

In his unfailing love, my God will stand
with me. He will let me look down
in triumph on all my enemies.

Psalm 59:10 nlt

Out of his fullness we have all received
grace in place of grace already given.

John 1:16 niv

The fruit of the Spirit is love, joy, peace,
forbearance, kindness, goodness, faithfulness,
gentleness and self-control.

Galatians 5:22–23 niv

Our trials are great opportunities.
Too often we look on them as great obstacles.
It would be a haven of rest and an inspiration
of unspeakable power if each of us from
now on would recognize every difficult
situation as one of God's chosen ways
of proving to us His love and look around
for the signals of His glorious manifestations;
then, indeed, would every cloud become
a rainbow and every mountain a path
of ascension and a scene of transfiguration.

A. B. SIMPSON

Each of us may be sure that if God sends us
on stony paths He will provide us with
strong shoes, and He will not send us out on
any journey for which He does not equip us well.

ALEXANDER MACLAREN

To be glad of life, because it gives you
the chance to love and to work and to play
and to look up at the stars; to be satisfied
with your possessions, but not contented with
yourself until you have made the best of them...
to think seldom of your enemies, often of your
friends, and every day of Christ; and to spend
as much time as you can, with body and with
spirit in God's out-of-doors—these are little
guideposts on the footpath to peace.

HENRY VAN DYKE

Clothe yourselves with love, which binds
us all together in perfect harmony. And let the
peace that comes from Christ rule in your hearts.

COLOSSIANS 3:14–15 NLT

But now the LORD my God has given
me peace on every side...and all is well.

1 KINGS 5:4 NLT

All perfect gifts are from above
and all our blessings show
The amplitude of God's dear love
which any heart may know.

LAURA LEE RANDALL

Blessed are all who fear the LORD,
who walk in obedience to him.

PSALM 128:1 NIV

Many of the richest blessings which
have come down to us from the past are the fruit
of sorrow or pain. We should never forget that
redemption, the world's greatest blessing,
is the fruit of the world's greatest sorrow.

MILLER

SEVEN

In Trials I Am Not Abandoned

"But I noticed that during the most trying periods of my life…"

ELLA H. SCHARRING-HAUSEN

I will let God's peace infuse every part of today.
As chaos swirls and life's demands pull
at me on all sides, I will breathe in God's peace
that surpasses all understanding.
He promised He would set within me
a peace too deeply planted to be affected
by unexpected or exhausting demands.

WENDY MOORE

Calm me, O Lord, as You stilled the storm,
Still me, O Lord, keep me from harm.
Let all the tumult within me cease,
Enfold me, Lord, in Your peace.

CELTIC TRADITIONAL

Don't fret or worry. Instead of worrying,
pray. Let petitions and praises shape your
worries into prayers, letting God know
your concerns. Before you know it, a sense of
God's wholeness, everything coming together
for good, will come and settle you down.
It's wonderful what happens when Christ
displaces worry at the center of your life.

PHILIPPIANS 4:6–7 MSG

When I can run to Jesus, when He is my refuge,
strength, and comforter, why would I fear
anything? There is no need for fear.
He is watching over me and that
sets my heart at peace.

God makes everything come out right;
  he puts victims back on their feet....
He doesn't treat us as our sins deserve,
  nor pay us back in full for our wrongs.
As high as heaven is over the earth,
  so strong is his love to those who fear him.
And as far as sunrise is from sunset,
  he has separated us from our sins.

PSALM 103:6, 9–12 MSG

God cannot give us a happiness
  and peace apart from Himself,
because it is not there. There is no such thing.

C. S. LEWIS

Yet the LORD longs to be gracious to you;
therefore he will rise to show you compassion.

ISAIAH 30:18 NIV

Lord, be gracious to us; we long for you.
Be our strength every morning,
our salvation in time of distress.

ISAIAH 33:2 NIV

Lord...give me only Your love and Your grace.
With this I am rich enough,
and I have no more to ask.

IGNATIUS OF LOYOLA

I will sing about your power.
Each morning I will sing with joy
about your unfailing love.
For you have been my refuge,
a place of safety when I am in distress.

PSALM 59:16 NLT

Whoever dwells in the shelter of the Most High
will rest in the shadow of the Almighty.

PSALM 91:1 NIV

The LORD is my light and my salvation—
whom shall I fear?
The LORD is the stronghold of my life—
of whom shall I be afraid?...
One thing I ask of the LORD, this only do I seek:
that I may dwell in the house of the LORD
all the days of my life,
to gaze upon the beauty of the LORD
and to seek him in his temple.
For in the day of trouble he will keep
me safe in his dwelling;
he will hide me in the shelter of his sacred tent
and set me high upon a rock....
Hear my voice when I call, LORD;
be merciful to me and answer me.

PSALM 27:1, 4–5, 7 NIV

There is no safer place to be
than in the Father's hands.

Leave behind your fear and dwell
on the lovingkindness of God, that you may
recover by gazing on Him.

Joy is the touch of God's finger. The object of
our longing is not the touch but the Toucher.
This is true of all good things—they are all
God's touch. Whatever we desire,
we are really desiring God.

PETER KREEFT

The godly will rejoice in the LORD
and find shelter in him.
And those who do what is right
will praise him.

PSALM 64:10 NLT

Every person's life is a fairy tale
written by God's fingers.

HANS CHRISTIAN ANDERSEN

Joy is really a road sign pointing us to God.
Once we have found God...we no longer need to
trouble ourselves so much about the quest for joy.

C. S. LEWIS

I will greatly rejoice in the LORD; my soul
will exult in my God, for He has clothed me
with the garments of salvation; He has wrapped
me with a robe of righteousness.

ISAIAH 61:10 NASB

Lift up your eyes. Your heavenly Father waits
to bless you—in inconceivable ways to make
your life what you never dreamed it could be.

ANNE ORTLUND

May the God of hope fill you with
all joy and peace in believing.

ROMANS 15:13 NKJV

I will lift up my eyes to the hills—
from whence comes my help?
My help comes from the Lord,
who made heaven and earth.
He will not allow your foot to be moved;
He who keeps you will not slumber.
Behold, He who keeps Israel
Shall neither slumber nor sleep.
The Lord is your keeper;
the Lord is your shade at your right hand.
The sun shall not strike you by day,
nor the moon by night.
The Lord shall preserve you from all evil;
He shall preserve your soul.
The Lord shall preserve
your going out and your coming in
from this time forth, and even forevermore.

Psalm 121:1–8 nkjv

Your deepest joy comes when you have nothing
around you to bring outward pleasure
and Jesus becomes your total joy.

A. Wetherell Johnson

Let us run with perseverance
the race marked out for us,
fixing our eyes on Jesus.... For the joy
set before him he endured the cross...
and sat down at the right hand
of the throne of God. Consider him
who endured...so that you will not
grow weary and lose heart.

HEBREWS 12:1–3 NIV

Be truly glad! There is wonderful joy ahead....
You love him even though you have never
seen him. Though you do not see him now,
you trust him; and you rejoice with a
glorious, inexpressible joy.

1 PETER 1:6, 8 NLT

Herein is joy, amid the ebb and flow of the
passing world: our God remains unmoved,
and His throne endures forever.

ROBERT COLEMAN

Those the LORD has rescued will return. They
will enter Zion with singing; everlasting joy will
crown their heads. Gladness and joy will overtake
them, and sorrow and sighing will flee away.

ISAIAH 35:10 NIV

Through all eternity to You
a joyful song I'll raise;
for oh! eternity's too short
to utter all Your praise.

JOSEPH ADDISON

Rejoice always, pray without ceasing,
in everything give thanks; for this is the will
of God in Christ Jesus for you.

1 THESSALONIANS 5:16–18 NKJV

Do not look forward to the changes
and chances of this life in fear; rather look
to them with full hope that, as they arise, God,
whose you are, will deliver you out of them.

FRANCIS DE SALES

Truly my soul finds rest in God;
my salvation comes from him.
Truly he is my rock and my salvation;
he is my fortress, I will never be shaken....
My salvation and my honor depend on God;
he is my mighty rock, my refuge.
Trust in him at all times, you people;
pour out your hearts to him,
for God is our refuge....
One thing God has spoken,
two things have I heard:
"Power belongs to you, God,
and with you, Lord, is unfailing love";
and, "You reward everyone according
to what they have done."

PSALM 62:1–2, 7–8, 11–12 NIV

As we follow Him who is everlasting
we will touch the things that last forever.

Joy comes from knowing God loves me
and knows who I am and where I'm going...that
my future is secure as I rest in Him.

JAMES DOBSON

Rest in the LORD, and wait patiently for Him.

PSALM 37:7 NASB

Abandon yourself to His care and guidance,
as a sheep in the care of a shepherd,
and trust Him utterly.

HANNAH WHITALL SMITH

Incredible as it may seem, God wants
our companionship. He wants to have
us close to Him. He wants to be a father to us,
to shield us, to protect us, to counsel us,
and to guide us in our way through life.

BILLY GRAHAM

The LORD will guide you always;
he will satisfy your needs in a sun-scorched land....
You will be like a well-watered garden,
like a spring whose waters never fail.

ISAIAH 58:11 NIV

Abandon yourself to His care and guidance,
as a sheep in the care of a shepherd,
and trust Him utterly.

HANNAH WHITALL SMITH

Through the heartfelt mercies of our God,
God's Sunrise will break in upon us...
showing us the way, one foot at a time,
down the path of peace.

LUKE 1:78–79 MSG

"Though the mountains be shaken and the hills be
removed, yet my unfailing love for you will not be
shaken nor my covenant of peace be removed,"
says the LORD, who has compassion on you.

ISAIAH 54:10 NIV

I will go before you and make the rough
places smooth; I will shatter the doors
of bronze and cut through their iron bars.

ISAIAH 45:2 NASB

His love has no limit, His grace has no measure,
His power no boundary known unto men;
For out of His infinite riches in Jesus
He giveth and giveth and giveth again.

ANNIE JOHNSON FLINT

Since you are my rock and my fortress,
for the sake of your name lead and guide me.

PSALM 31:2–3 NIV

GOD...rekindles burned-out lives with fresh hope,
restoring dignity and respect to their lives—
a place in the sun! For the very structures
of earth are GOD'S; he has laid out
his operations on a firm foundation.

1 SAMUEL 2:7–8 MSG

EIGHT

When I Don't Understand

"I have needed You..."

ELLA H. SCHARRING-HAUSEN

God has put into each of our lives a void that
cannot be filled by the world. We may leave
God or put Him on hold, but He is always there,
patiently waiting for us...to turn back to Him.

EMILIE BARNES

As for me, I trust in You, O LORD. I say,
"You are my God." My times are in Your hand.

PSALM 31:14–15 NASB

God is waiting for us to come to Him with our
needs.... God's throne room is always open.

CHARLES STANLEY

It's usually through our hard times, the
unexpected and not-according-to-plan times,
that we experience God in more intimate ways.
We discover an unquenchable longing to know
Him more. It's a passion that isn't concerned that
life fall within certain predictable lines,
but a passion that pursues God and knows
He is relentless in His pursuit of each one of us.

WENDY MOORE

God waits to give to those who ask Him
a wisdom that will bind us to Himself,
a wisdom that will find expression in a spirit
of faith and a life of faithfulness.

J. I. PACKER

God waits for us in the inner sanctuary
of the soul. He welcomes us there.

RICHARD J. FOSTER

Don't you see how wonderfully kind,
tolerant, and patient God is with you?...
Can't you see that his kindness is intended
to turn you from your sin?

ROMANS 2:4 NLT

In difficulties, I can drink freely of God's
power and experience His touch
of refreshment and blessing—much like
an invigorating early spring rain.

ANABEL GILLHAM

Lord, you have been our dwelling place
throughout all generations.
Before the mountains were born or you
brought forth the whole world,
from everlasting to everlasting you are God.

PSALM 90:1–2 NIV

Before me, even as behind, God is, and all is well.

JOHN GREENLEAF WHITTIER

A living, loving God can and does
make His presence felt, can and does
speak to us in the silence of our hearts,
can and does warm and caress us till we
no longer doubt that He is near, that He is here.

BRENNAN MANNING

We walk without fear, full of hope and courage
and strength to do His will, waiting for the
endless good which He is always giving as fast as
He can get us able to take it in.

GEORGE MACDONALD

Open your mouth and taste, open your eyes and
see—how good GOD is. Blessed are you who
run to him. Worship GOD if you want the best;
worship opens doors to all his goodness.

PSALM 34:8–9 MSG

The goodness of God is infinitely
more wonderful than we will ever
be able to comprehend.

A. W. TOZER

All that is good, all that is true,
all that is beautiful, all that is beneficent,
be it great or small, be it perfect
or fragmentary, natural as well
as supernatural, moral as well as material,
comes from God.

JOHN HENRY NEWMAN

I am still confident in this:
I will see the goodness of the LORD
in the land of the living.
Wait for the LORD;
be strong and take heart
and wait for the LORD.

PSALM 27:13–14 NIV

The simple fact of being...
in the presence of the Lord
and of showing Him all that I think, feel,
sense, and experience, without trying
to hide anything, must please Him.
Somehow, somewhere, I know that
He loves me, even though I do not feel
that love as I can feel a human embrace,
even though I do not hear a voice
as I hear human words of consolation....
God is greater than my senses,
greater than my thoughts,
greater than my heart. I do believe
that He touches me in places
that are unknown even to myself.

HENRI J. M. NOUWEN

But He knows the way I take;
When He has tried me,
I shall come forth as gold.

JOB 23:10 NASB

Pour out your heart to God your Father.
He understands you better than you do.
It is in silence that God is known,
and through mysteries that He declares Himself.

ROBERT H. BENSON

You, O God, are both tender and kind,
not easily angered, immense in love,
and you never, never quit.

PSALM 86:15 MSG

In His love He clothes us, enfolds us,
and embraces us; that tender love completely
surrounds us, never to leave us.

JULIAN OF NORWICH

The LORD is merciful and compassionate,
slow to get angry and filled with unfailing love....
The LORD always keeps his promises;
he is gracious in all he does.

PSALM 145:8, 13 NLT

This is your Father you are dealing with,
and he knows better than you what you need.
With a God like this loving you,
you can pray very simply.

MATTHEW 6:7 MSG

If anyone loves God, this one is known by Him.

1 CORINTHIANS 8:3 NKJV

You are valuable just because you exist.
Not because of what you do or what you have
done, but simply because you are. Just think
about the way Jesus honors you...and smile.

MAX LUCADO

We have come to know and have believed
the love which God has for us. God is love,
and the one who abides in love abides in God,
and God abides in him.

1 JOHN 4:16 NASB

For God so loved the world that he gave
his one and only Son, that whoever believes
in him shall not perish but have eternal life.

JOHN 3:16 NIV

You are no stranger to God. He planned
for you…from before the foundation
of the world, and His plan was to be with you.
And He invites you to realize it, to come
into a continual awareness of His presence
and be revolutionized by it.

RAY AND ANNE ORTLUND

Even when all we see are the tangled threads
on the backside of life's tapestry, we know that
God is good and is out to do us good always.

RICHARD FOSTER

"For I know the plans I have for you," declares the LORD, "plans to prosper you and not to harm you, plans to give you hope and a future."

JEREMIAH 29:11 NIV

Know you not that day follows night, that flood comes after ebb, that spring and summer succeed winter? Hope you then! Hope you ever!
God fails you not.

CHARLES H. SPURGEON

God provides resting places as well as working places. Rest, then, and be thankful when He brings you, wearied to a wayside well.

L. B. COWMAN

No eye has seen, no ear has heard, no mind has imagined what God has prepared for those who love him.

1 CORINTHIANS 2:9 NLT

In those times I can't seem to find God,
I rest in the assurance He knows how to find me.

NEVA COYLE

This is what the LORD says:
"Stand at the crossroads and look;
ask for the ancient paths,
ask where the good way is, and walk in it,
and you will find rest for your souls."

JEREMIAH 6:16 NIV

Rest. Rest in God's love. The only work you
are required now to do is to give your inmost
intense attention to His still, small voice within.

MADAME JEANNE GUYON

God's peace is joy resting.
His joy is peace dancing.

F. F. BRUCE

Perhaps this moment is unclear,
but let it be—even if the next, and many
moments after that are unclear,
let them be. Trust that God
will help you work them out,
and that all the unclear
moments will bring you
to that moment of clarity
and action when you are known
by Him and know Him.
These are the better
and brighter moments of His blessing.

WENDY MOORE

The temptations in your life
are no different from what
others experience. And God is faithful.
He will not allow the temptation
to be more than you can stand.
When you are tempted, he will show
you a way out so that you can endure.

1 CORINTHIANS 10:13 NLT

But do not let this one fact escape your notice, beloved.... The Lord is not slow about His promise, as some count slowness, but is patient toward you, not wishing for any to perish but for all to come to repentance.

2 PETER 3:8–9 NASB

Give me a word, O Word of the Father: touch my heart: enlighten the understandings of my heart: open my lips and fill them with Your praise.

LANCELOT ANDREWES

If any of you lacks wisdom, let him ask of God, who gives to all generously and without reproach, and it will be given to him.

JAMES 1:5 NASB

Strength, rest, guidance, grace, help, sympathy, love—all from God to us! What a list of blessings!

EVELYN STENBOCK

Show the wonders of your great love....
Keep me as the apple of your eye;
hide me in the shadow of your wings.

PSALM 17:7–8 NIV

At the very heart and foundation
of all God's dealings with us, however dark
and mysterious they may be, we must dare
to believe in and assert the infinite, unmerited,
and unchanging love of God.

All the things in this world are gifts
and signs of God's love to us.
The whole world is a love letter from God.

PETER KREEFT

The hope we have in Christ is an absolute
certainty. We can be sure that the place Christ
is preparing for us will be ready when we arrive,
because with Him nothing is left to chance.
Everything He promised He will deliver.

BILLY GRAHAM

"One set of footprints is when I carried you...."

ELLA H. SCHARRING-HAUSEN

Look back from where we have come....
How could we know the joy without the
suffering? And how could we endure the
suffering but that we are warmed
and carried on the breast of God?

DESMOND M. TUTU

Let the beloved of the LORD rest secure in him,
for he shields him all day long, and the one the
LORD loves rests between his shoulders.

DEUTERONOMY 33:12 NIV

There is the whisper of His love,
the joy of His presence,
and the shining of His face,
for those who love Jesus for Himself alone.

SUSAN B. STRACHAN

Where can I go from your Spirit?
Where can I flee from your presence?
If I go up to the heavens, you are there;
if I make my bed in the depths, you are there.
If I rise on the wings of the dawn,
if I settle on the far side of the sea,
even there your hand will guide me,
your right hand will hold me fast.

PSALM 139:7–10 NIV

O Lord God, in whom we live, and move,
and have our being, open our eyes that
we may behold Your fatherly presence ever
about us. Draw our hearts to Yourself
with the power of Your love.

BROOKE FOSS WESTCOTT

I am with you and will watch over you
wherever you go.

GENESIS 28:15 NIV

I pray that you,
being rooted and established in love,
may have power, together with all the Lord's
holy people, to grasp how wide and long
and high and deep is the love of Christ,
and to know this love
that surpasses knowledge—
that you may be filled to the measure
of all the fullness of God.
Now to him who is able to do
immeasurably more
than all we ask or imagine,
according to his power that is
at work within us, to him be glory
in the church and in Christ Jesus
throughout all generations, for ever and ever!
Amen.

EPHESIANS 3:17–21 NIV

Look for, long for, pray for, and expect special
breaking-through times when God makes
His presence very real, very powerful!
And until they come, dwell in His presence
by faith and gaze upon His beauty.

RAY AND ANNE ORTLUND

God longs to give favor—that is, spiritual
strength and health—to those who seek Him,
and Him alone. He grants spiritual favors
and victories...in order to make His holy beauty
and His great redeeming power known.

TERESA OF AVILA

God is working in you, giving you the desire
and the power to do what pleases him.

PHILIPPIANS 2:13 NLT

Among our treasures are such wonderful
things as the grace of Christ, the love of Christ,
the joy and peace of Christ.

L. B. COWMAN

God guides us,
despite our uncertainties and our vagueness,
even through our failings and mistakes....
He leads us step by step,
from event to event.
Only afterwards, as we look back
over the way we have come
and reconsider certain
important moments in our lives
in the light of all that has followed them,
or when we survey
the whole progress of our lives,
do we experience the feeling of
having been led without knowing it,
the feeling that God
has mysteriously guided us.

PAUL TOURNIER

Let us then approach the throne of God's grace
with confidence, so that we may receive mercy
and find grace to help us in our time of need.

HEBREWS 4:16 NIV

Yea, though I walk through the valley
of the shadow of death,
I will fear no evil; for You are with me;
Your rod and Your staff, they comfort me.
You prepare a table before me
in the presence of my enemies;
You anoint my head with oil; my cup runs over.
Surely goodness and mercy shall follow me
All the days of my life:
And I will dwell in the house of the LORD forever.

PSALM 23:4–6 NKJV

They travel lightly whom God's grace carries.

THOMAS À KEMPIS

You carry us, and You go before,
You are the journey, and the journey's end.

BOETHIUS

Today Jesus is working just as wonderful works as when He created the heaven and the earth. His wondrous grace, His wonderful omnipotence, is for His child who needs Him and who trusts Him, even today.

CHARLES E. HURLBURT AND T. C. HORTON

The God who created, names, and numbers the stars in the heavens also numbers the hairs of my head.... He pays attention to very big things and to very small ones. What matters to me matters to Him, and that changes my life.

ELISABETH ELLIOT

In all their distress he too was distressed, and the angel of his presence saved them. In his love and mercy he redeemed them; he lifted them up and carried them all the days of old.

ISAIAH 63:9 NIV

In comparison with this big world,
the human heart is only a small thing. Though
the world is so large, it is utterly unable to satisfy
this tiny heart. Our ever growing soul and its
capacities can be satisfied only in the infinite
God. As water is restless until it reaches its level,
so the soul has no peace until it rests in God.

SADHU SUNDAR SINGH

He tends his flock like a shepherd:
He gathers the lambs in his arms
and carries them close to his heart.

ISAIAH 40:11 NIV

In His arms He carries you all day long.

FANNY J. CROSBY

I am the good shepherd. The good shepherd
gives His life for the sheep.

JOHN 10:11 NKJV

What matters supremely is not the fact that
I know God, but the larger fact which
underlies it—the fact that He knows me.
I am graven on the palms of His hands. I am
never out of His mind. All my knowledge of
Him depends on His sustained initiative in
knowing me. I know Him because He first
knew me, and continues to know me.

J. I. PACKER

God has a wonderful plan for each
person He has chosen. He knew even
before He created this world what beauty
He would bring forth from our lives.

LOUISE B. WYLY

You're blessed when you feel you've lost what
is most dear to you. Only then can you be
embraced by the One most dear to you.

MATTHEW 5:4 MSG

God walks with us…. He scoops us up in His
arms or simply sits with us in silent strength
until we cannot avoid the awesome recognition
that yes, even now, He is here.

GLORIA GAITHER

I will remember that when I give Him my heart,
God chooses to live within me—body and soul.
And I know He really is as close as breathing,
His very Spirit inside of me.

There's not a tint that paints the rose
Or decks the lily fair,
Or marks the humblest flower that grows,
But God has placed it there….
There's not a place on earth's vast round,
In ocean's deep or air,
Where love and beauty are not found,
For God is everywhere.

God is our refuge and strength, an ever-present
help in trouble. Therefore we will not fear.

PSALM 46:1–2 NIV

At every moment, God is calling your name and
waiting to be found. To each cry of "Oh Lord,"
God answers, "I am here."

God is the sunshine that warms us, the rain
that melts the frost and waters the young plants.
The presence of God is a climate of strong and
bracing love, always there.

JOAN ARNOLD

The more we depend on God the more
dependable we find He is.

CLIFF RICHARD

You have made known to me the path of life;
you will fill me with joy in your presence,
with eternal pleasures at your right hand.

PSALM 16:11 NIV

The LORD your God is with you,
the Mighty Warrior who saves.
He will take great delight in you;
in his love he will not longer rebuke you,
but will rejoice over you with singing.

ZEPHANIAH 3:17 NIV

Tonight I will sleep beneath Your feet,
O Lord of the mountains and valleys,
ruler of the trees and vines. I will rest
in Your love, with You protecting me as a father
protects his children, with You watching over
me as a mother watches over her children.

Long before he laid down earth's foundations,
he had us in mind, had settled on us
as the focus of his love.... It's in Christ
that we find out who we are and what we
are living for. Long before we first heard
of Christ and got our hopes up, he had his
eye on us, had designs on us for glorious living.

EPHESIANS 1:4, 11 MSG

He is everything that is good and comfortable
for us. He is our clothing that for love wraps us,
clasps us, and all surrounds us for tender love.

JULIAN OF NORWICH

When we allow God the privilege of shaping
our lives, we discover new depths of purpose
and meaning. What a joyful thought to realize
you are a chosen vessel for God—
perfectly suited for His use.

JOANI EARECKSON TADA

We have been in God's thought from
all eternity, and in His creative love,
His attention never leaves us.

MICHAEL QUOIST

The Lord doesn't always remove the sources
of stress in our lives...but He's always there
and cares for us. We can feel His arms
around us on the darkest night.

JAMES DOBSON

God's way is perfect. All the LORD's promises
prove true. He is a shield for all
who look to him for protection.

PSALM 18:30 NLT

The light of God surrounds me,
The love of God enfolds me....
The presence of God watches over me,
Wherever I am, God is.

What can harm us when everything must first
touch God whose presence surrounds us?

Nothing enters your life accidently—
remember that. Behind our every experience
is our loving, sovereign God.

CHARLES R. SWINDOLL

The LORD is my strength and my shield;
my heart trusted in Him, and I am helped.

PSALM 28:7 NKJV

There is no need to plead that the love
of God shall fill our hearts as though He
were unwilling to fill us.... Love is pressing
around us on all sides like air. Cease to resist
it and instantly love takes possession.

AMY CARMICHAEL

God's love is meteoric, his loyalty astronomic,
His purpose titanic, his verdicts oceanic.
Yet in his largeness nothing gets lost.

PSALM 36:5 MSG

This is how love is made complete
among us so that we will have confidence
on the day of judgment: In this world
we are like Jesus. There is no fear in love.
But perfect love drives out fear.

1 JOHN 4:17–18 NIV

The eternal God is your refuge,
and underneath are the everlasting arms.

DEUTERONOMY 33:27 NKJV

He is the Rock, his works are perfect,
and all his ways are just. A faithful God
who does no wrong, upright and just is he.

DEUTERONOMY 32:4 NIV

May you experience the love of Christ,
though it is too great to understand fully.
Then you will be made complete with all the
fullness of life and power that comes from God.

EPHESIANS 3:19 NLT

You carry us, and You go before,
You are the journey, and the journey's end.

BOETHIUS

God takes care of His own. He knows our
needs.... He stands ready to come to our rescue.
And at just the right moment He steps in and
proves Himself as our faithful heavenly Father.

CHARLES R. SWINDOLL

I've called your name. You're mine.
When you're in over your head,
I'll be there with you.
When you're in rough waters,
you will not go down.
When you're between a rock and a hard place,
it won't be a dead end—
Because I am GOD, your personal God,
The Holy of Israel, your Savior.
I paid a huge price for you...!
That's how much you mean to me!
That's how much I love you!

ISAIAH 43:1–4 MSG

With God our trust can be abandoned, utterly
free. In Him are no limitations, no flaws,
no weaknesses. His judgment is perfect, His
knowledge of us is perfect, His love is perfect.
God alone is trustworthy.

EUGENIA PRICE

An Invitation

If you have ever:

    questioned if this is all there is to life...

    wondered what happens when you die...

    felt a longing for purpose or significance...

    wrestled with resurfacing anger...

    struggled to forgive someone...

    known there is a "higher power" but couldn't define it...

    sensed you have a role to play in the world...

    experienced success and still felt empty afterward...

then consider Jesus.

A great teacher from two millennia ago, Jesus of Nazareth, the Son of God, freely chose to show our Maker's everlasting love for us by offering to take all of our flaws, darkness, death, and mistakes into His very body (1 Peter 2:24). The result was His death on a cross. But the story doesn't end there. God raised Him from the dead and invites us to believe this truth in our hearts and follow Jesus into eternal life.

If you confess with your mouth that Jesus is Lord and believe in your heart that God raised him from the dead, you will be saved. —ROMANS 10:9 NLT